Rattlesnakes

Written by Jessica Lee Anderson

Photos by Bob Ferguson II

Paperback ISBN: 978-1-964078-19-9

To everyone who works to conserve and protect wildlife, including the misunderstood and often feared. - JLA

To my wife and best friend, Julie. Much like rattlesnakes, I am in awe of your flawless design and power, all while bringing purpose and joy to my life. - BF

All photos taken by Bob Ferguson II apart from P. 16: Mark Kostich (Eastern Diamondback skull); P. 32: Michael Anderson and Phil Dunning

Names of species (current iNaturalist common names) clockwise from top left, unless otherwise noted: Front cover: Prairie Rattlesnake; Cover page: Carolina Pygmy Rattlesnake; Dedication: Central American Rattlesnake; P. 4: Yucatán Neotropical Rattlesnake; P. 5: Banded Rock Rattlesnake; P. 6: Southern Pacific Rattlesnake, Banded Rock Rattlesnake, Carolina (Sandhills) Pygmy Rattlesnake, Yucatán Neotropical Rattlesnake; P. 7: Eastern Diamondback Rattlesnake, Carolina Pygmy Rattlesnake; P. 8: Sonoran Sidewinder Rattlesnake, Timber (Canebrake) Rattlesnake; P. 9: Southern Speckled Rattlesnake, Southern Pacific Rattlesnake; P. 10: Western Diamondback baby, Timber Rattlesnake, Carolina Pygmy Rattlesnake, Speckled Rattlesnake; P. 11: Eastern Diamondback Rattlesnake, Southern Speckled Rattlesnake, Timber Rattlesnake, Great Basin Rattlesnake; P. 12: Timber Rattlesnakes; P. 13: Timber Rattlesnake; P. 14: Mojave Rattlesnake; P. 15: Timber Rattlesnake, Dusky Pygmy Rattlesnake; P. 16: Eastern Diamondback; P. 17: Timber Rattlesnake, Red Diamond Rattlesnake; P. 18: Prairie Rattlesnake, Western Diamondback Rattlesnake; P. 19: Southern Speckled Rattlesnake; P. 20: Southern Pacific Rattlesnake; P. 21: Timber Rattlesnakes; P. 22: Timber Rattlesnake; P. 23: Timber Rattlesnake; P. 24: Timber Rattlesnakes; P. 25: Timber Rattlesnake, Carolina (Sandhills) Pygmy Rattlesnake; P. 26: Timber Rattlesnake, Western Diamondback Rattlesnake; P. 27: Timber Rattlesnake, Southern Speckled Rattlesnake, Timber Rattlesnake; P. 28: Western Diamondback Rattlesnake; P. 29: Timber Rattlesnake with Eastern Copperhead, Timber Rattlesnakes; P. 30: Timber Rattlesnake giving birth, P. 31: Timber Rattlesnake mother with babies, Mojave Rattlesnake baby tail; P. 32: Timber Rattlesnakes; P. 33: Panamint Rattlesnake; Back cover: Timber Rattlesnake

This Book Belongs to:

_____

Rattlesnakes are venomous reptiles that fall into two different groups—*Crotalus* and *Sistrurus*. They are known as pit vipers because they have heat-sensing pits between their eyes and nostrils. These pit organs create a "heat-picture" (sort of like a night vision camera).

Rattlesnakes get their name from the rattles at the end of their tails. The rattles are made of keratin (the same protein that forms your skin and hair). When rattlesnakes sense danger, they can vibrate their tails to make a rattling noise to warn potential threats.

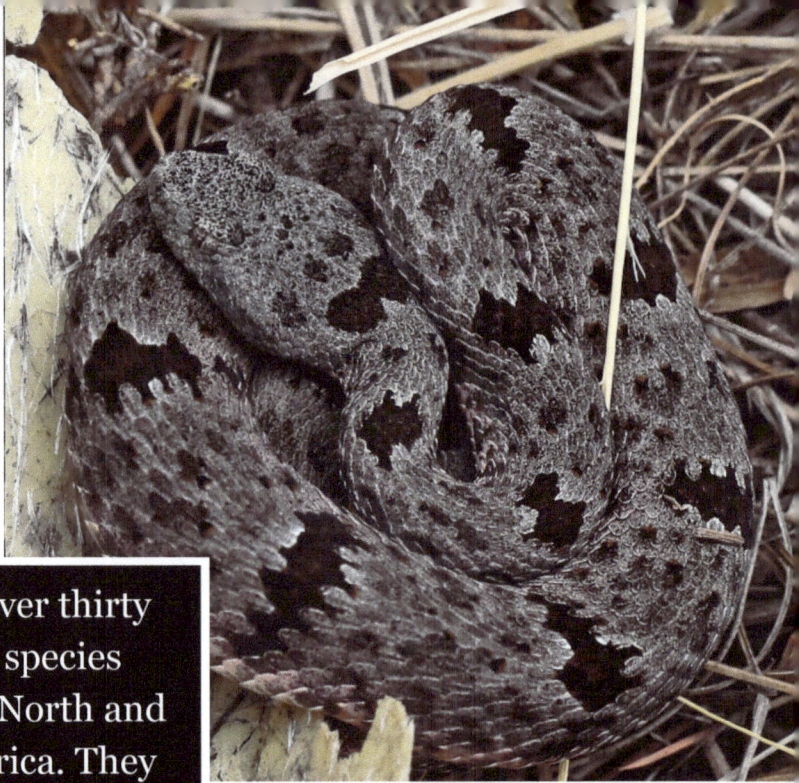

There are over thirty rattlesnake species that live in North and South America. They range from as far north as Canada to as far south as Argentina.

Rattlesnake species tend to be heavy-bodied and large, though some smaller species exist. They range from 14 inches (.4 m) to 5-8 feet long (1.5-2.4 m).

Rattlesnakes live in a variety of habitats, such as deserts, plains, forests, and swamps. Many species live near rocky areas because the rocks provide shelter and a source of food (prey like lizards and rodents also dwell near the rocks).

The body temperature of rattlesnakes and all reptiles varies. This is why they're called "cold-blooded" (though biologists will often use the term poikilothermic instead). Rattlesnakes will bask on rocks because the sun raises their body temperature.

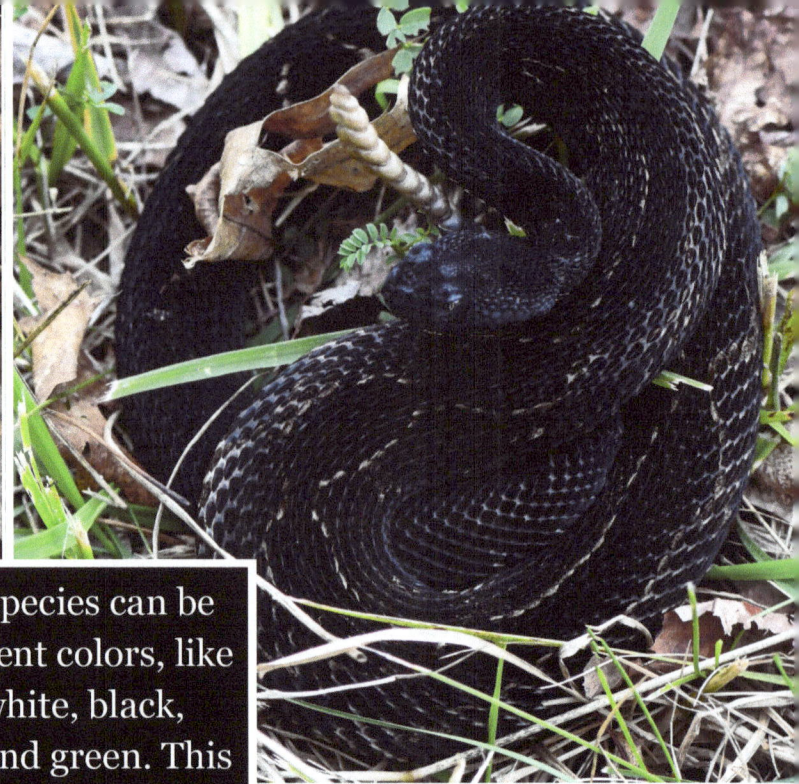

Rattlesnake species can be several different colors, like brown, tan, white, black, red, yellow, and green. This helps them blend into their environment (camouflage). As some species age, their coloring might change (such as turning darker).

They can have different patterns, such as speckles, blotches, diamonds, and chevrons (V-shaped patterns). Patterns also help snakes camouflage, which is important when hunting prey and avoiding potential predators.

Even in the same rattlesnake species, colors and patterns can vary greatly!

Rattlesnakes have keeled scales, meaning a ridge runs down the center of the scales. Keeled scales give rattlesnakes a dry, rough look. Their special skin structures help them survive harsh conditions by collecting rain, sleet, and snow. They'll coil to gather the water and then sip what they collect.

Like all kinds of snakes, rattlesnakes locate prey by scent, but they smell a different way than humans do. Their forked tongues flick in and out to pick up smells using a smell sensor called the Jacobson's organ.

Rattlesnakes will often lie in wait for prey to come close. They have fangs that fold flat inside their mouth until they're ready to strike—then they spring out, sort of like a pocketknife.

Rattlesnake skull

Rattlesnake fangs are hollow and sharp like a needle, and they get replaced regularly throughout the snake's lifetime. Fangs inject venom—a toxic secretion that can stun, kill, and kickstart digestion.

Rattlesnake venom is made of proteins and chemicals. Venom can be extracted to make medications to include antivenom (antivenin) that treats snakebites. Rattlesnakes store their venom in glands that are located behind and below their eyes (which gives their heads a wide appearance).

If rattlesnakes sense danger, they might hide or coil up, often getting in the shape of the letter "S" to look bigger and more intimidating. They might hiss or rattle a warning so they will be left alone.

If their posture, hissing, and rattling is not enough to scare an attacker away, a rattlesnake might bite in defense. Venom takes effort for a rattlesnake to produce, so they can choose to not waste it by delivering a dry bite (meaning they don't inject venom).

Researchers have found that larger rattlesnakes have the possibility to inject more venom because they have larger venom stores. The amount of venom injected can also vary based on the circumstances of the bite (for example, a rattlesnake might use less venom trying to get a threat to back off compared to using more if it gets attacked).

Rattlesnakes don't hunt people or seek them out. To avoid snakebites, leave snakes alone and give them space (especially if they try to escape or hide). Wear shoes while hiking in nature, stay on paths and trails, and avoid reaching into areas you can't see.

Rattlesnakes hunt prey like frogs, birds, lizards, and rodents during the day and at night, swallowing their meals whole. They can survive for months without eating. Younger snakes eat more often than fully grown adults, and they eat smaller prey items until they grow bigger and have the ability to eat larger prey.

Rattlesnakes help the overall health of an ecosystem by keeping the population of certain mammals like rodents in check. If unbalanced, disease might spread and/or plant species might get wiped out. Snakes also serve as a source of food for other creatures such as hawks, owls, coyotes, and even other snakes.

It can take some rattlesnakes a week or more to digest dinner depending on the size of the prey eaten as well as the outside temperature since their bodies will slow down in the cold. Many rattlesnakes spend winters piled up together in a den. A group of rattlesnakes is called a rhumba.

Rattlesnakes play another important role in the environment by spreading plant seeds! Because rattlesnakes don't chew, the seeds that their prey once ate can stay whole inside the snake's body. The seeds can even start to sprout in a snake's colon before the snake poops them out, sometimes in a spot miles away.

Rattlesnakes shed their skin throughout their lives, and during this time, their eyes appear blue as fluid gathers between the old layer of skin and the new layer of skin. With every shed, rattlesnakes add another segment to their rattle. You can't tell how old a snake is by the number of segments —some snakes shed multiple times a year, plus segments can break off.

Rattlesnakes have clear eyelids that don't move. Their pupils (the center part of the eye) are elliptical, or cat-like, allowing them to see in dim environments.

Snakes don't have all the same ear parts that you do, but they can sense vibrations and certain sounds. Besides hissing and rattling, rattlesnakes have another form of communication: using chemical signals called pheromones to find a mate.

Researchers are continuing to learn more about rattlesnakes, like discovering that they are social and will seek the company of some snakes . . . while avoiding others. Some rattlesnake species hang out in social cliques called nodes.

Female rattlesnakes don't lay eggs like some other kinds of snakes—they give birth to live young. While rattlesnake babies have fangs that can inject venom, they remain vulnerable because of their small size.

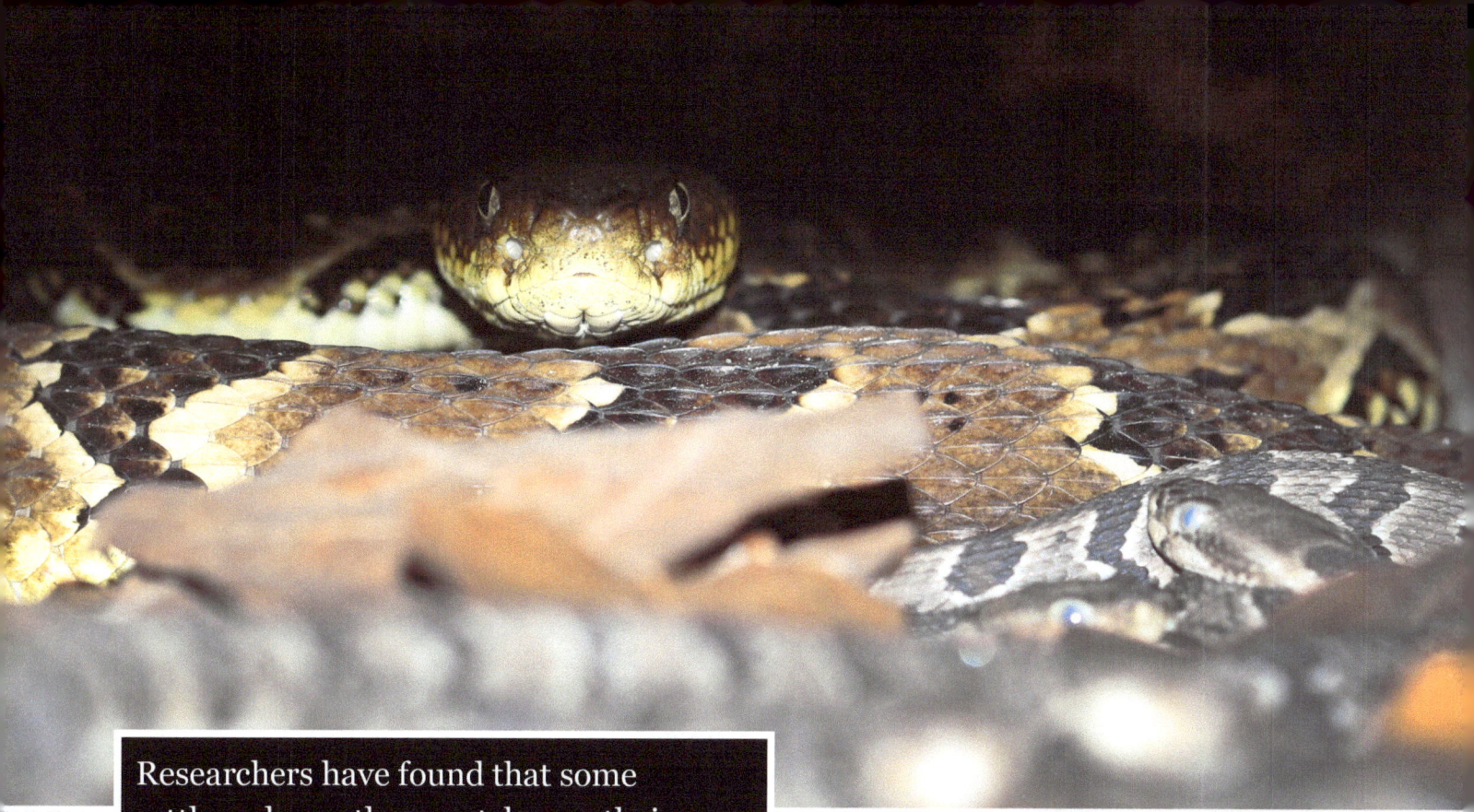

Researchers have found that some rattlesnake mothers watch over their babies until the little snakelets shed their skin for the first time. The babies have a small knob at the end of their tail called a button that will lengthen and develop into a rattle as the babies continue to shed.

Rattlesnakes live on average between 10 to 25 years with some living well over 30 years (even longer in captivity). Rattlesnakes and other snake species can get diseases like snake fungal disease, an infection caused by a fungus. Some species are on the decline because of habitat loss and being hunted for events like rattlesnake roundups.

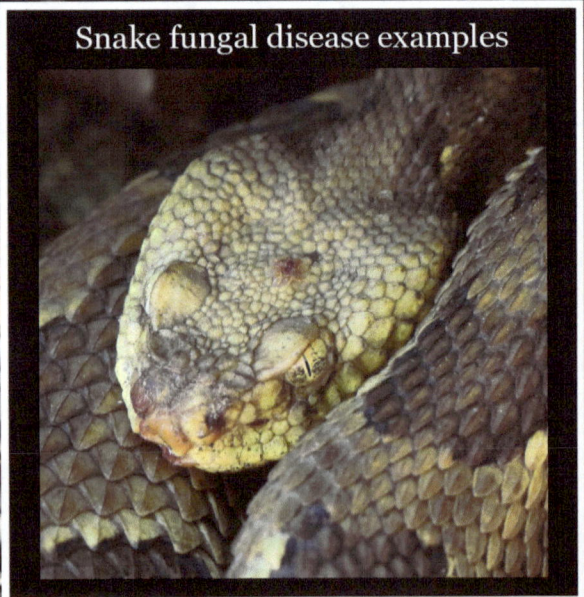

Snake fungal disease examples

Rattlesnakes are often feared and misunderstood, though they are an important part of nature. They have some remarkable, unique features that set them apart from other snake species.

Jessica Lee Anderson is an award-winning author of over 75 books for young readers including the NAOMI NASH chapter book series. Jessica loves spending time in nature and exploring the outdoors with her husband, Michael, and their daughter, Ava! Jessica was once afraid of rattlesnakes after her young niece was envenomed (and thankfully was okay!). Jessica now has a deep appreciation for them. You can learn more about Jessica by visiting www.jessicaleeanderson.com.

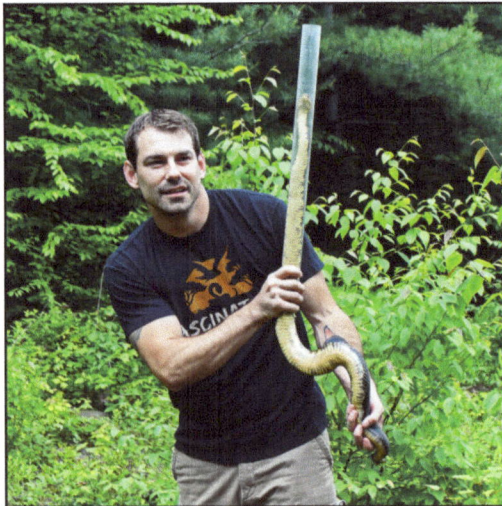

Bob is a naturalist with a compulsion to be outdoors. Wildlife conservation through entertainment, education, fundraising, and fieldwork is his mission and purpose in life. His organization, Fascinature, has donated six figures to saving land in the world's most biodiverse spaces. He even has a frog named after him! You can find him on Instagram @bob_ferguson_fascinature or sign up for his newsletter at fascinature.live.

Check out these other books:

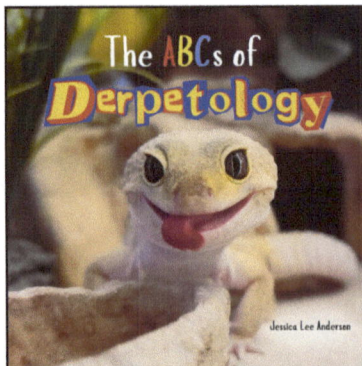

The ABCs of Derpetology

Jessica Lee Anderson

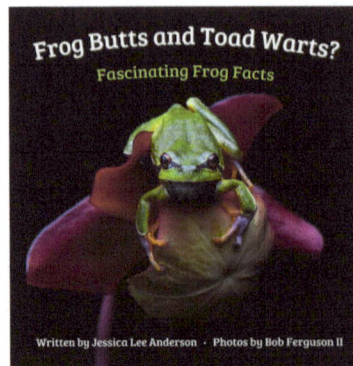

Frog Butts and Toad Warts?
Fascinating Frog Facts

Written by Jessica Lee Anderson · Photos by Bob Ferguson II

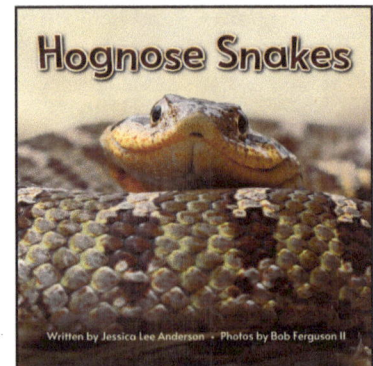

Hognose Snakes

Written by Jessica Lee Anderson · Photos by Bob Ferguson II

www.ingramcontent.com/pod-product-compliance
Lightning Source LLC
Chambersburg PA
CBHW061145030426
42335CB00002B/108

9781964078199